ARMIES OF THE PAST

GOING TO WAR IN
ROMAN
TIMES

GOING TO WAR IN
ROMAN
TIMES

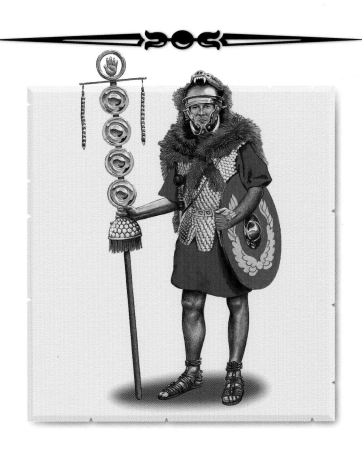

MOIRA BUTTERFIELD

W
FRANKLIN WATTS
LONDON•SYDNEY

⊙ **ILLUSTRATIONS BY**
Mark Bergin,
Giovanni Caselli,
Chris Molan,
Lee Montgomery,
Peter Visscher.
Maps by Hardlines

This edition 2003

Franklin Watts
96 Leonard Street
London EC2A 4XD

Franklin Watts Australia
45-51 Huntley Street
Alexandria
NSW 2015

© 2000 Franklin Watts

Editor Penny Clarke
Editor-in-Chief John C. Miles

Designer Steve Prosser
Art Director Jonathan Hair

ISBN 0 7496 5173 3

Dewey classification: 937

A CIP catalogue record
for this book is available
from the British Library.

Printed in Hong Kong, China

CONTENTS

THE ROMAN ARMY

Roman civilisation began hundreds of years before the birth of Christ in the area now called Italy. Over the next thousand years the Roman Empire controlled many parts of Europe and North Africa.

The secret of the Empire's success was its strong army, which conquered new lands and defended the Empire's frontiers from attack. At first ordinary Romans were called up to fight, but later the army became professional. It contained the best-trained soldiers in the ancient world.

Vallum Hadriani (Hadrian's Wall)

Conquest of Britain AD34–83

Deva

Londinium

BRITANNIA (now Britain)

OCEANUS ATLANTICUS (Atlantic Ocean)

Lutetia

GAUL (now France)

Julius Caesar conquers Gaul 58-51BC

Massilia

HISPANIA (now Spain)

Italica

Gades

Carthago Nova

 The Roman Empire

 Major settlements

 Military campaigns

Bronze statue of Romulus, Remus and the she-wolf

Founding of Rome 509BC
Legend has it that Rome was founded by Romulus and Remus, who were raised by a she-wolf.

Julius Caesar 100–44BC
Julius Caesar fought many important battles during his reign as Roman ruler. He even visited Britain.

Claudians 30BC–AD69
This famous dynasty was founded by the Emperor Augustus.

Augustus, the first Roman Emperor

The Roman Empire

This map shows the Roman Empire in AD117, at its largest and most powerful. It stretched from northern England south-east to Egypt. The map also shows some important military events that took place during the Empire's thousand-year history.

GERMANIA (now Germany)

Campaigns along the Rhine and Danube 17BC–AD16

Dacian campaign AD101–106

Civil Wars 49–30BC

DACIA (now Romania)

ILLYRICUM

Salonae

THRACIA (now part of Turkey)

PONTUS EUXINUS (Black Sea)

ITALIA (now Italy)

Constantinople

ARMENIA

Roma

MACEDONIA (Greece)

Punic Wars 264–146BC

Pergamum

Campaigns in the East AD113–117

Athenae

SICILIA (now Sicily)

Corinthus

Carthago

Syracusae

MESOPOTAMIA

MARE INTERNUM (Mediterranean)

JUDAEA

Leptis Magna

Petra

Alexandria

The Jewish rebellion AD66–73

AFRICA

The Palace of Diocletian

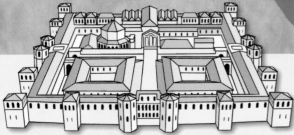

The Roman Empire AD117
The Empire was at its largest in the reign of Emperor Trajan.

The Empire splits AD286
Under the Emperor Diocletian the Roman Empire was split into two, East and West.

Fall of Rome AD410
Ancient Rome was destroyed by German tribes. Constantinople (now Istanbul) became the capital of what remained of the Empire.

LEGIONS

The Roman army was organised into groups of soldiers called legions. Each legion had a name, number, badge and main fortress base. There were roughly 30 legions in all, posted around the frontiers of the Roman Empire.

A legion was self-sufficient, which meant it had all the men it needed to build forts, fight battles and look after its troops. It had its own commanders, lower-ranking officers, ordinary soldiers and people with special skills such as engineers and doctors.

STANDARDS
Each legion had its own standards – poles with badges on them.

THE STRUCTURE OF A LEGION

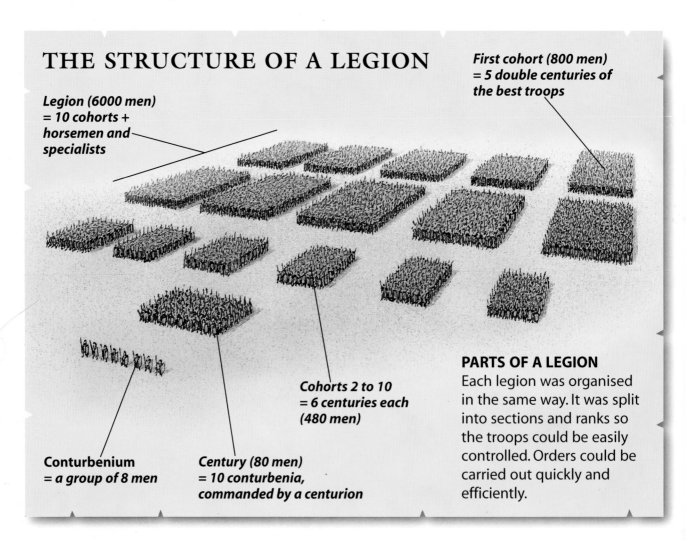

Legion (6000 men)
= 10 cohorts + horsemen and specialists

First cohort (800 men)
= 5 double centuries of the best troops

Conturbenium
= a group of 8 men

Century (80 men)
= 10 conturbenia, commanded by a centurion

Cohorts 2 to 10
= 6 centuries each (480 men)

PARTS OF A LEGION
Each legion was organised in the same way. It was split into sections and ranks so the troops could be easily controlled. Orders could be carried out quickly and efficiently.

A LEGION'S RANKS

Within the legion there was a strict system of ranks. Recruits started their careers as ordinary legionaries. They then worked their way up by promotion.

Eventually a legionary could become a centurion and perhaps one day rise to *praefectus castrorum*, second-in-command of the entire legion.

> '*Do not forget, Roman, that your special talent is to rule other people.*'
>
> **Virgil, Roman poet**

 AT THE TOP

The legate and his six officers, the tribunes, came from Rome's most aristocratic families. They served short spells in the army before becoming governors of important provinces.

WHO WAS WHO

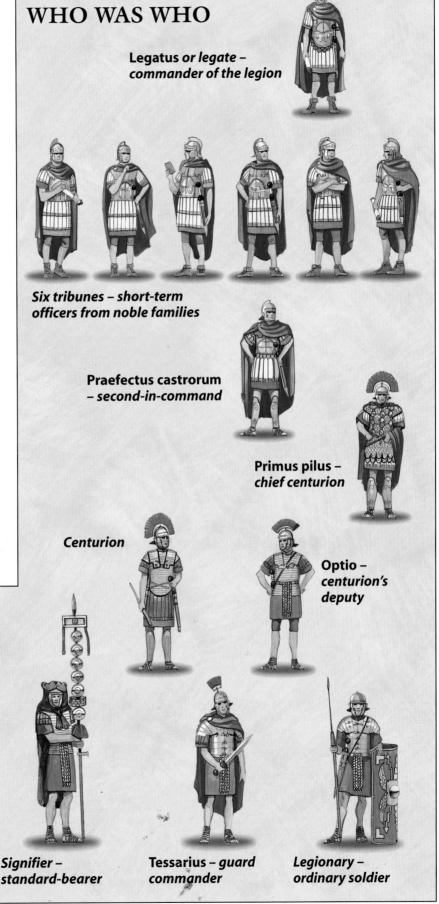

Legatus *or* legate – *commander of the legion*

Six tribunes – short-term officers from noble families

Praefectus castrorum – second-in-command

Primus pilus – *chief centurion*

Centurion

Optio – *centurion's deputy*

Auxiliary – soldier who was not a Roman citizen

Signifier – standard-bearer

Tessarius – *guard commander*

Legionary – ordinary soldier

JOIN THE ARMY!

If you wanted to join the Roman army you would have to be a male Roman citizen at least 18 years old and 1.7 metres tall, healthy and of good character. It would help if you could get someone important to write explaining what a fine person you were.

You would be sent for an interview and given a medical. If you were accepted, you signed up for twenty-five years. You would be posted to a legion and asked to take an oath of loyalty to the Emperor of Rome.

I PROMISE . . .
Soldiers raised one hand when they took the oath of loyalty.

ARMY PAY

Denarii coins

PAY DAYS
A legionary's basic pay was about 300 *denarii* (silver pieces) per year. Some pay was held back for food and equipment, pension and funeral savings. The balance was paid out roughly every three months.

WHY JOIN?
In the army a recruit learned skills and was well fed. Not only did he earn money, he travelled with the legion to far-off lands and could comfortably retire after his service.

1 denarius bought 25 oysters

25 denarii = one shirt

WHERE THE MONEY WENT

Pension   **Spending**

Funeral club   **Food and equipment**

SPENDING
Legionaries' pay did not go far. In about AD100 a new shirt cost about a month's pay.

IN TRAINING

New recruits went through a thorough training, not just in fighting but also in skills such as roadbuilding, carpentry and even swimming.

The troops went on regular manoeuvres, including cross-country marches and overnight camping trips.

KILL!

Recruits learned to fight by attacking wooden posts with wooden swords, javelins and wicker shields while a centurion shouted instructions at them.

ON PARADE

Every morning (twice a day for new recruits) legionaries would go to the parade ground to practise marching patterns, battle formations and responding to commands.

'Make sure your army commander notices your short hair, hairy nostrils and broad shoulders . . . That way you might become a centurion by the time you're sixty.'

Juvenal, Roman poet

A centurion watches troops in training

ARMOUR AND WEAPONS

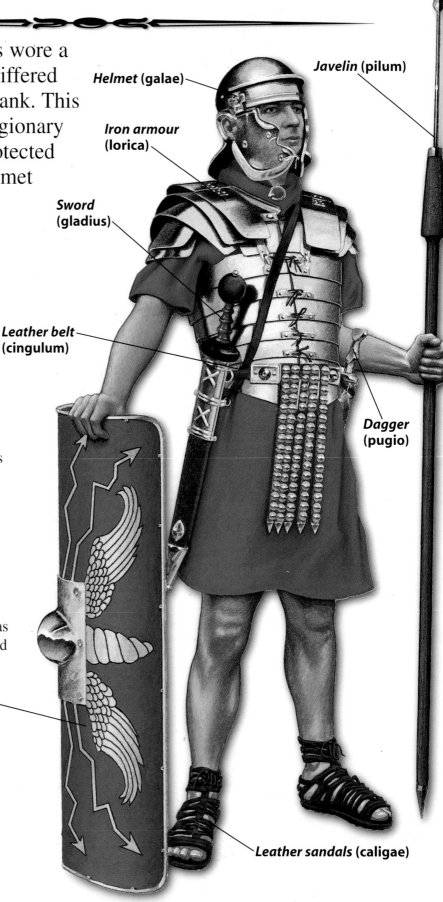

Helmet (galae)

Javelin (pilum)

Iron armour (lorica)

Sword (gladius)

Leather belt (cingulum)

Dagger (pugio)

Shield (scutum)

Leather sandals (caligae)

All Roman soldiers wore a uniform, which differed in style according to rank. This is what an ordinary legionary wore. His uniform protected him in battle – the helmet had cheek pieces to protect his face and a guard at the back to protect his neck. The body armour was flexible to allow movement.

 **EQUIPMENT**

In the picture on the right, a legionary displays his basic equipment. Like all the soldiers in this book, he dates from the time when the Roman Empire was at its largest – AD117.

ARMOUR

Body armour was made of overlapping iron strips held together by leather straps. It was heavy but comfortable and good at deflecting sword blows.

TUNIC AND SHOES

Under their armour legionaries wore a woollen tunic and a linen undershirt. The leather sandals had hobnails in the soles so they would not wear out on long marches.

WEAPONS

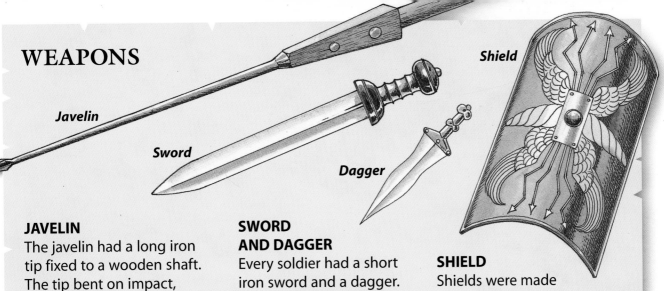

Javelin

Sword

Dagger

Shield

JAVELIN
The javelin had a long iron tip fixed to a wooden shaft. The tip bent on impact, making it very difficult for the enemy to pull the javelin out of the ground or a shield once it had stuck in.

SWORD AND DAGGER
Every soldier had a short iron sword and a dagger. They both had sharp points designed for stabbing the enemy at close range.

SHIELD
Shields were made from sheets of wood glued together and covered in leather or linen. They had a metal boss in the middle.

STANDARD-BEARERS
Every century also had its own standard, which was always carried by a soldier called a signifier. He wore a bearskin and a shirt made of brass scales.

The most important standard of all showed a golden eagle (*aquila* in Latin). The man who carried it was called the *aquilifer*.

Oath hand

SIGNIFIER

Legion's badge

'During the battle a cowardly aquilifer ran off, leaving Julius Caesar himself holding the aquila.'

Roman scholar Suetonius

AUXILIARIES

The legions also employed auxiliaries. These were soldiers born in other lands who were not Roman citizens. They wore a different uniform to the legionaries. This could include a chain-mail shirt and sometimes trousers. They had flat oval shields that were brightly decorated and they carried stabbing spears.

Auxiliaries often had special skills, such as horse-riding and archery, and they played an important part in many of Rome's greatest victories.

AUXILIARY ARCHER

Stabbing spear (hasta)

Chain mail

Oval shield

AUXILIARY FOOT SOLDIER

Chain-mail shirt

GOOD SCOUTS
Auxiliary troops included light infantry – fast-moving, lightly armed foot soldiers – and cavalry, who fought on horseback. Both were frequently used as scouts or border patrols.

FIRE!
Auxiliary archers and slingers (slingshot experts) fired arrows and catapulted stones at the enemy during a battle.

AN AUXILIARY'S LIFE

AWAY FROM HOME
Auxiliary units were often posted far from home so they would be less likely to change sides in a battle, or have to fight their own friends and relatives.

ALL AT SEA
There was a Roman navy, but Roman-born soldiers traditionally hated the sea. Recruits from seafaring provinces made better naval crews.

INTO RETIREMENT
At the end of his career an auxiliary was awarded Roman citizenship, a great honour that he could pass on to his children. He could retire and perhaps buy a farm in the country.

ON HORSEBACK
Auxiliary cavalry units, called *ala*, trained in skills such as jumping on to a moving horse and hitting a target while galloping. This must have been difficult because stirrups were unknown in Roman times.

SHOWING OFF
Sometimes the cavalry put on riding displays for the rest of the legion. Then they wore decorated armour and gilt helmets with face-masks.

An auxiliary cavalryman displays his skills

FORTS

Legions were stationed in fortresses, which were protected by thick walls and had gates guarded by sentries. Inside the walls there were lots of buildings, such as barracks for the soldiers, houses for the officers, food and equipment stores, carpentry workshops, bathhouses and hospital rooms.

Outside the walls there was usually a settlement of civilians (non-army personnel) who worked in the fortress or ran shops and taverns used by the soldiers.

SUPPER TIME

Soldiers cooked on a stove with a griddle on top, like a modern barbecue. To their basic food rations they added spices and olive oil brought by the legion from Rome.

SECTION THROUGH A BARRACK ROOM

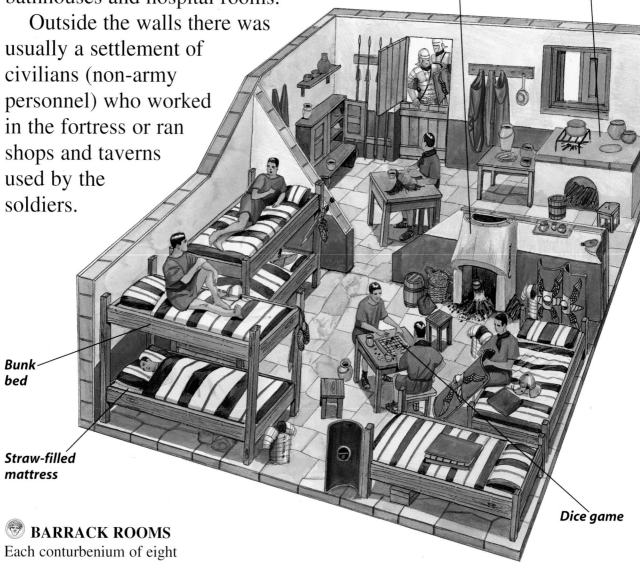

Fireplace

Kitchen area

Bunk bed

Straw-filled mattress

Dice game

BARRACK ROOMS

Each conturbenium of eight men had a barrack room to share between them. They slept on bunks with straw-filled mattresses. The soldiers could relax in their barrack room, playing dice, cleaning their armour and perhaps taking turns doing the cooking with rations collected from the fortress's stores.

CENTURION

The centurion had his own rooms nearby, so he could keep a check on his soldiers.

BIG AND SMALL

Fortresses were big enough for a whole legion but there were also smaller forts that could house a cohort, and some small lookout posts for just a few soldiers. Soldiers on the march slept in tents set up in overnight camps.

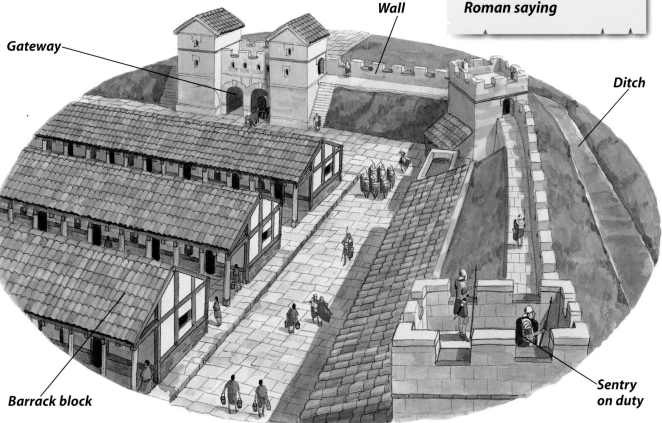

Gateway

Wall

Ditch

Barrack block

Sentry on duty

FORTRESS LIFE

FORTRESS CHORES
When they weren't training or doing sentry duty, legionaries had daily chores such as sweeping their barrack rooms.

BATH TIME
Each fortress had its own bathhouse where the soldiers could swim, exercise, bath and be massaged with oil by slaves.

FAMILY LIFE
Soldiers could not marry but they often had girlfriends and children living in the settlement next to their base.

On the March

When the legion was on the move the soldiers had to march at a rate of approximately six kilometres an hour for five hours at a time. They carried about 14 kilograms of weapons and armour, plus 18 kilograms of extra kit.

Centurions kept an eye on the soldiers and hit them if they lagged behind. Each night the troops stopped and built a temporary camp that they could defend if they were attacked. They slept in tents, one for each conturbenium.

 ON THE MARCH

Each legionary carried his equipment on a pole. This included his food rations, cooking utensils, tools and two stakes to help build a palisade (wooden wall) around the camp.

KEEP ORDER!
Legions marched in strict order, each rank in its place.

Legionary on the march

MAKING CAMP

SURVEYING
All campsites were laid out to the same plan. Once a site had been chosen, surveyors measured and marked out a rectangle.

DIGGING
While some soldiers stayed on sentry duty watching for enemies, others dug a ditch and piled the earth up into a bank around the campsite.

ALMOST READY
On top of the bank, legionaries used their stakes to construct a palisade. Then the soldiers put their tents up inside, in straight, well-ordered lines.

AMBUSHED!

When legions were marching in an extended line, they had to beware in case an enemy ambushed them. To stop this happening scouts went ahead of the main band of troops, commanders and standards marched in the centre, and at the back was a strong rearguard of cavalry and infantry.

'He would often beat his head on a door, shouting: "Quinctilius Varus, give me back my legions!"'

Suetonius writing about the Emperor Augustus after the massacre in AD9

BRITISH ATTACK

In AD60 rebel British forces ambushed and destroyed part of the Ninth Legion on its way to defend Londinium (London).

LOST LEGIONS

The worst ambush was in AD9, when three legions under the command of Varus were massacred in the Black Forest, Germany. They were probably ambushed while building their camp. Nobody knew what had happened to them until later expeditions found piles of bones.

INTO BATTLE

In battle, the Roman army lined up in a strict order, and every soldier was trained to fight in the same way. Legionaries were in the middle at the front, with reserve troops behind them. Auxiliaries were situated on either side. This order and discipline helped the Romans to beat enemies such as the Celts, whose forces were not so well trained or disciplined.

A COMMON BATTLE FORMATION

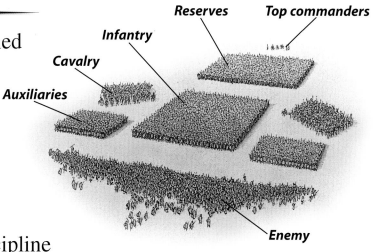

Reserves

Top commanders

Infantry

Cavalry

Auxiliaries

Enemy

GOOD PLANNING
Battle formations were carefully planned by the commanders.

BATTLE TACTICS

JAVELIN SKILLS
Throw one; then march towards the enemy and throw another.

AUXILIARY ACTION
Fire on the enemy with slingshots, bows and arrows.

STAB LOW
In hand-to-hand combat, fight by stabbing with your sword.

USE YOUR SHIELD
Use your shield as a weapon, bashing it upwards at the enemy.

LEFT-HANDERS
Left-handed troops fight together in a special section.

OBEY ORDERS
Always do what your centurion says. If you don't, you'll be killed.

FORMATIONS

SQUARE

If the enemy surrounded a group of soldiers, the troops formed a square. They were protected by their interlocked shields, with their javelins sticking out.

Pig's head

THE TORTOISE

If a group of soldiers wanted to attack an enemy fort, they put their shields above their heads to protect themselves from missiles hurled from the walls by the defenders.

Square

PIG'S HEAD

Soldiers practised fighting in formations. The wedge-shaped 'pig's head' smashed into a lined-up enemy, pushing them down with a wall of shields.

Tortoise

BATTLE MORALE

In battle, a horn-player called a *cornicen* gave signals. For instance, the troops might be called to rally around their standard, which they could see above the groups of fighting men.

There was also a special standard called the *imago* with the emperor's face on it. This showed that he was symbolically fighting with his troops. This was meant to keep the legionaries' spirits up even in the midst of the fiercest fighting.

Standard-bearer holding the imago

Army horn-player (cornicen)

Siege!

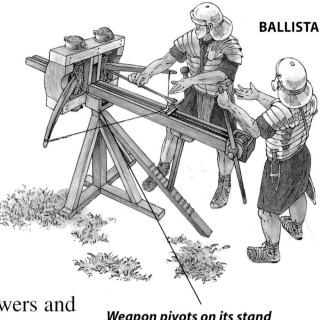

BALLISTA

When the Roman army invaded new lands it often encountered an enemy hiding inside a walled town or fortress. Then the Roman troops had to lay siege, starving the enemy into surrender or trying to break through the defences.

The legions usually had the advantage because they possessed towers and ladders for climbing walls, and machinery for firing missiles such as iron-tipped arrows or big heavy boulders.

Weapon pivots on its stand

BALLISTA

The ballista was a catapult used in battles and sieges to fire shot or bolts (arrows) up to 70 centimetres long. It could pivot on its stand to allow aiming.

CATAPULTA

Each century had a catapulta that fired small bolts with armour-piercing iron tips. It was nicknamed 'the scorpion' because its arrows were as sharp as a scorpion's sting.

Arm springs up

Sling

Rock

ONAGER

ONAGER

Each cohort had a siege engine called an onager. This fired big rocks in a wide arc. Each rock was loaded into a sling on the end of an arm powered by twisted ropes.

Winch draws back the bowstring

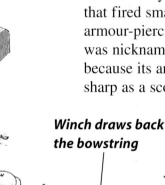

CATAPULTA

REACHING THE TOP

If the army needed to scale high walls they built wooden siege towers and trundled them forwards into position. Then troops climbed them, protected from the enemy's missiles. During long sieges, the Romans sometimes built huge ramps of timber, earth and rubble to reach the top of the enemy's walls.

CLIMBING HEROES

The first soldier to scale an enemy wall was honoured as a hero, given a gold crown and a money prize. His family got the award if he was killed.

'Vespasian gave the order to demolish the city, but there were few left alive to care.'

Historian Josephus on the victory at Jotapata

BLOODY VICTORY

In AD66 the Romans besieged the city of Jotapata in the Middle East. They used giant battering rams to crack the walls and also built a huge earth ramp to reach the top.

The enemy poured boiling oil on them but finally the Romans won and the soldiers massacred everyone inside. The Roman army could be bloodthirsty and extremely brutal, especially when a siege was successful.

AFTER THE BATTLE

Each legion had its own doctors and medical assistants, who did what they could to help soldiers on the battlefield. They also cared for sick troops in the hospital wing of a fortress.

Roman doctors used herbs as medicine, and each hospital had its own herb garden. The herbs were dried, crushed and mixed into ointments or potions.

Although Roman doctors could not perform internal surgery, they knew a lot about natural remedies. For instance, they collected turpentine, the resin from a pine tree, and rubbed it into wounds to stop them becoming infected.

AMPUTATIONS

If a leg or an arm was badly injured it was usually amputated (cut off).

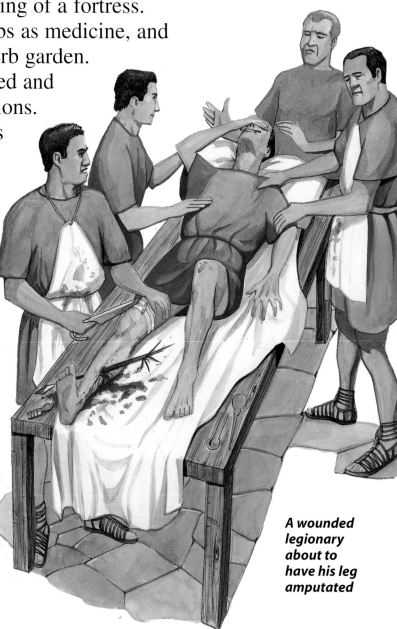

A wounded legionary about to have his leg amputated

FOR BRUISES

If a soldier had bruises and sprains the doctor usually smeared on a paste made from a herb called comfrey, and then gave the soldier a herbal drink to swallow.

KILL OR CURE

For more painful treatments, such as tooth removal or amputations, there was no anaesthetic. The doctor probably gave the patient lots of wine to dull the pain and then got helpers to hold him down on a table.

TRIUMPHAL MARCH

Legions that had taken part in a successful campaign might be allowed a triumph – a march through Rome, cheered on by huge crowds. Captured treasure and prisoners were paraded as well. At the end of the triumph the most important prisoner would be publicly strangled.

Victorious commander

Prisoner

Standard

Captured treasure

'I came, I saw, I conquered!'

Roman general Julius Caesar

PRAETORIAN GUARD

Apart from triumphal marches, the legions were kept out of Rome, in case they decided to revolt against the emperor. The only soldiers allowed in Rome were the Praetorian Guard. These experienced troops acted as the emperor's own bodyguard. The Praetorians were notorious bullies who sometimes even murdered the emperor himself.

GODS AND BELIEFS

The Romans worshipped many gods and goddesses who were believed to look down from their home high up on heavenly Mount Olympus. If the gods were displeased terrible things could happen, so the Romans regularly made animal sacrifices to keep the gods happy.

Army commanders were no different. They worshipped and made sacrifices before a battle, and in each fortress there was a temple to Mars, god of war.

Statue of Mars

MARS WILL DECIDE

Romans believed that Mars decided who won, who lost and who died in battle. Soldiers prayed to him for protection and victory, and offered him the spoils of war after a success. Statues of Mars usually show him wearing armour, ready for battle.

Offerings to the gods

SACRIFICES

Romans sacrificed domestic animals, such as bulls, sheep and pigs, on temple altars. They offered the animals to the gods as a kind of heavenly food. In return they asked the gods for favours. They wrote their requests on pieces of lead and threw them into special sacred underground springs and wells, asking the gods to punish their enemies or to grant special wishes.

MITHRAISM

Around the 1st century BC Mithraism became a popular religion in the army. Soldiers worshipped the god Mithras in hidden underground temples. They also sacrificed bulls to him. The soldiers believed that doing this would ensure them a happy afterlife if they died a violent death in battle.

A temple dedicated to Mithras

BURIALS AND SUPERSTITIONS

Burial urn

PIPED OFFERINGS
Occasionally a pipe led from the surface of the ground down to a soldier's buried ashes. Visitors to the burial site poured wine or oil down the pipe.

Plaque to scare off evil spirits

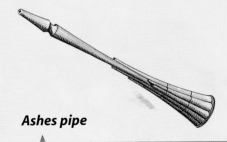

MILITARY BURIALS
A dead soldier's body was usually cremated (burned) and his ashes buried in an urn. Sometimes jars of oil or wine were buried to sustain him on his after-life journey.

Ashes pipe

SUPERSTITIONS
Like all Romans, soldiers were superstitious. They carried lucky charms and put plaques on walls to scare off evil spirits.

END OF THE EMPIRE

After hundreds of years, the Roman Empire began to break up. It was too large to defend properly, and its leaders in Rome spent too much time fighting each other. In AD410 the city of Rome was attacked by barbarian tribes from Germany, but there was no one strong enough to save the city.

However, before the city fell the Empire had been divided. The eastern part was ruled from a new capital called Constantinople. This new empire became very important. Historians call it the Byzantine Empire.

ROME IN RUINS
The invaders destroyed Rome's great buildings and treasures.

CHRISTIANITY

The Bible was copied into Latin

RELIGIOUS CHANGES
At first Christians were not tolerated in Rome, but this ended when the Emperor Constantine became a Christian around AD312.

CHURCH LANGUAGE
Latin, the language of the Romans, survived the break-up of the Empire because it became the language of the Christian church.

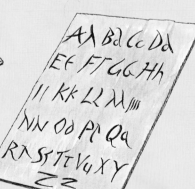

The old Roman alphabet

The Christian Emperor Justinian

EASTERN EMPERORS
The rulers of the Byzantine Empire were Christian. They followed the teachings of the Bible and called themselves Holy Roman Emperors.

WHAT IS LEFT?

There are lots of Roman remains that you can still see. Fortresses and campsites survive all over Europe and North Africa, and archaeologists have excavated equipment such as helmets, swords and pieces of armour. There are invisible remains, too. On retirement many soldiers settled in the lands where they were serving. They would have had families, and perhaps their descendants are still living in those countries today.

Scabbard

Legionary helmet

Sword blade

ARCHAEOLOGICAL FINDS

'Time is like a strong river. No sooner does something appear than it is swept away and replaced by something else.'

Emperor Marcus Aurelius

WALK THE WALL

Far away from Rome, in northern Britain, you can still walk Hadrian's Wall as if you were a Roman soldier on the lookout for enemies. The wall was begun in AD121 to defend Rome's northernmost frontier. The soldiers patrolled the wall wearing their shiny armour, carrying their javelins and shields, certain that the Roman Empire, which they would spend 25 years of their lives serving, would go on for ever.

Hadrian's Wall

GLOSSARY

Ala
Groups of auxiliary cavalry soldiers.

Aquila
The most sacred standard of the legion, with a golden eagle on the top.

Aquilifer
The soldier who carried the aquila.

Auxiliary
Soldier who was not a Roman citizen.

Legionary standard

Ballista
Giant catapult on a wooden frame.

Centurion
Soldier of a legion in charge of a century (80 men).

Century
Group of 80 men who fought together; commanded by a centurion.

Cingulum
Soldier's leather belt that carried a dagger and a groin-protector made of studded leather straps.

Citizen
A free Roman; for non-Romans to be given Roman citizenship was a great honour.

Cohort
Section of a legion. There were ten cohorts in total.

Conturbenium
A legion's smallest section; eight men who lived, worked and fought together.

Cornicen
The legion's horn player. Horns were used to make signals during battle.

Statue of Mars

Denarius
Roman coin used to pay soldiers.

Fortress
Fort large enough for a whole legion to live in.

Galae
Soldier's iron or brass helmet.

Gladius
Soldier's short stabbing sword, worn in a scabbard on the right-hand side.

Imago
A special standard with the image of the emperor on it.

Legate
The man in command of a whole legion.

Legionary
Ordinary foot soldier.

Lorica
Armour made of metal strips laced together at the front and back.

Marching camp
Overnight camp dug and built by soldiers on the move.

Mars
The Roman god of war.

Burial urn

Mithraism
Roman military religion, involving bull-sacrifice and worship of the sun god Mithras.

Onager
Siege engine that fired boulders at the enemy.

Optio
A centurion's second-in-command.

Pilum
Javelin with a wooden shaft and a sharp iron tip.

Pugio
Sharp iron dagger carried in a decorated scabbard on the left-hand side.

Scutum
Rectangular shield made of wood encased in leather.

Signifier
Soldier who carried a standard.

Standard
Long pole with the legion's badges and symbols on it. In battle it was a rallying point for the soldiers.

Plaque for scaring away evil spirits

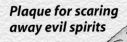

Tribune
Legionary officer ranked below a legate. Tribunes were high-born Romans.

Triumph
A ceremonial march through Rome, granted to legions when they won great campaigns.

Auxiliary foot soldier

INDEX

A
amputation 24
aquila/aquilifer 13, 30
archaeology 29
archers 14
armour 12–13, 14, 15, 16, 18, 26, 29
auxiliaries 9, 14–15, 20, 30

B
barracks 16, 17
bathhouses 16, 17
battle 8, 14, 15, 20–21, 22, 26, 27
battle formation 11, 20, 21
Britain 6, 29
burial 10, 27
Byzantine Empire 28

C
Caesar, Julius 6
camps 17, 18, 19, 29, 31
cavalry 8, 14, 15, 19, 31
centuries 8, 13, 22, 30
centurions 8, 9, 11, 16, 18, 20, 30, 31
Christianity 28
citizens, Roman 9, 14, 15, 30
cohorts 8, 17, 22, 30
Constantinople 6, 7, 28
conturbenium 8, 16, 18, 30

D
denarius 10, 30
doctors 8, 24

E
emperors, Roman 6, 10, 21, 25, 28, 31
Europe 6, 29

F
families 15, 17, 23, 29
fighting 11; see also battles
food 10, 16, 18
forts and fortresses 8, 16–17, 21, 24, 26, 27, 29, 30

G
Germany 7, 19, 28
gods 26–27

H
Hadrian's Wall 6, 29
Holy Roman Emperors 28
horn player 21, 30
hospitals 16, 24

I
imago 21, 31
infantry 14, 19
Italy 6, 7

L
Latin 28
legate 9, 30, 31
legionaries 9, 11, 12–13, 16, 17, 20, 30, 31
legions 8–9, 10, 14, 15, 16, 18, 19, 20–21, 22, 24, 25, 30, 31

M
marches/marching 11, 12, 18–19, 28, 31
Mars, god of war 26, 31
medicines 24
Mithras, sun god 27, 31

O
officers 8, 16
optio 9, 31

P
parades 11
pay 10
Praetorian Guard 25
prisoners 25

R
recruits 9, 10–11
religion 26–27, 28
Roman Empire 6–7, 8, 28–29
Rome, city of 6, 7, 9, 16, 25, 28, 29, 31

S
sacrifices to gods 26, 27
scouts 14, 19
sentries 16, 17, 18
sieges 21, 22–23
signifier 9, 13, 31
standard-bearer 9, 13, 21
standards 8, 13, 19, 21, 31

T
tents 17, 18
training 10–11, 17
tribunes 9, 31
triumph 25, 31

U
uniforms 12, 14

W
weapons 11, 12–13, 14–15, 18, 20–21, 22–23, 29, 30, 31